TRANSCENDING RACE IN AMERICA
BIOGRAPHIES OF BIRACIAL ACHIEVERS

Halle Berry

Beyoncé

David Blaine

Mariah Carey

Frederick Douglass

W. E. B. Du Bois

Salma Hayek

Derek Jeter

Alicia Keys

Soledad O'Brien

Rosa Parks

Prince

Booker T. Washington

SOLEDAD O'BRIEN

Television Journalist

David Robson

Mason Crest Publishers

Produced by 21st Century Publishing and Communications, Inc.

MASON CREST PUBLISHERS INC.
370 Reed Road
Broomall, Pennsylvania 19008
(866) MCP-BOOK (toll free)
www.masoncrest.com

Printed in the United States of America.

First Printing

9 8 7 6 5 4 3 2 1

Library of Congress Cataloging-in-Publication Data

Robson, David, 1966–
    Soledad O'Brien / David Robson.
        p. cm. — (Transcending race in America)
    Includes bibliographical references and index.
    Includes webliography.
    ISBN 978-1-4222-1617-0 (hardback : alk. paper) — ISBN 978-1-4222-1631-6 (pbk. : alk. paper)
    1. O'Brien, Soledad, 1966–   —Juvenile literature. 2. Television journalists—United States—Biography—Juvenile literature. 3. African American television journalists—Biography—Juvenile literature. 4. Women television journalists—United States—Biography.—Juvenile literature. I. Title.
PN4874.O355R63 2009
070'.92—dc22
[B]   2009024024

Table of Contents

> **❝** I have brothers, sisters, nieces, nephews, uncles, and cousins, of every race and every hue, scattered across three continents, and for as long as I live, I will never forget that in no other country on Earth is my story even possible. **❞**

> **❝** We may have different stories, but we hold common hopes. . . . We may not look the same and we may not have come from the same place, but we all want to move in the same direction — towards a better future . . . **❞**

— Barack Obama, 44th President
of the United States of America

7

Chapter

1

❀

NOW, IT'S PERSONAL

IN EARLY 2008, REPORTER SOLEDAD O'BRIEN took an amazing journey. In nearly 20 years as a broadcaster she had covered hundreds of stories. But none seemed as personal and as vital as this one. Over a series of months, Soledad traveled across the United States to report about the lives of African Americans for a new documentary called *Black in America*.

From Maine to Florida, North Carolina to California, Soledad and her camera crew sought to capture the lives of black Americans in the 21st century. The year 2008 marked 40 years since the death of civil rights icon Dr. Martin Luther King, Jr. The program took a look at the progress and setbacks people of color had experienced since that fateful April day. The first episode in the series investigated King's assassination itself.

Beyond King's murder, *Black in America* took an honest look at contemporary African-American experience. Soledad talked to

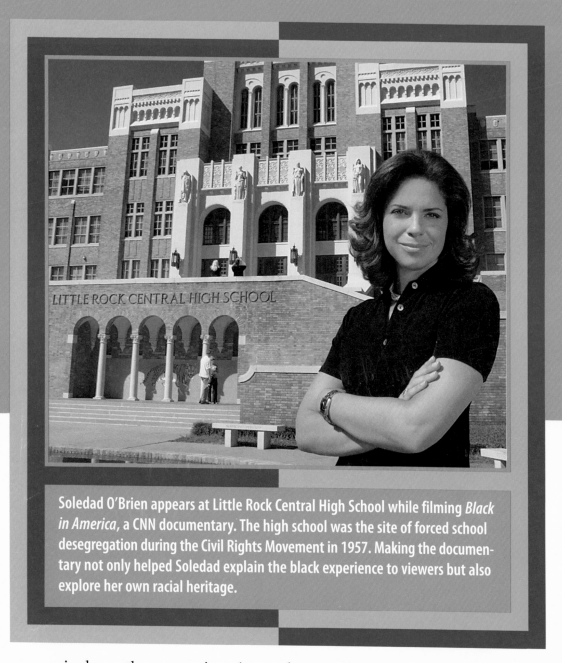

Soledad O'Brien appears at Little Rock Central High School while filming *Black in America,* a CNN documentary. The high school was the site of forced school desegregation during the Civil Rights Movement in 1957. Making the documentary not only helped Soledad explain the black experience to viewers but also explore her own racial heritage.

single mothers, men in prisons, those suffering from **HIV/AIDS**, and others struggling to make ends meet.

A DEEPER TRUTH

Upon its debut in July 2008, critics praised the program as important. Among other things, critic Tom Shales singled out Soledad's skills as an interviewer:

FROM SOLEDAD O'BRIEN
WHO BROUGHT YOU
THE CRITICALLY ACCLAIMED

CNN PRESENTS
EYEWITNESS TO
MURDER
THE KING ASSASSINATION

"A GROUNDBREAKING
DOCUMENTARY SERIES"
— Kimberly C. Roberts,
The Philadelphia Tribune

"BLOWN AWAY
IN APPRECIATION"
— Areyla J. Mitchell, The Mid-South Tribune

"UNEARTHS
INTERESTING TWISTS"
— Milton Allimadi, The Black Star

"INVITES VIEWERS
TO REACH
THEIR OWN
CONCLUSION..."
— Ashley Chaney, Essence Magazine

"FASCINATING
REASSESSMENT"
— Neil Genzlinger, The New York Times

BLACK IN AMERICA
REPORTED BY SOLEDAD O'BRIEN

Soledad's impartial and engaging interview skills in the *Black in America* series
won praise from critics. She was pleased that her professionalism was recognized,
but as a biracial woman, she felt a deep connection to the program that went
beyond her job as a reporter.

"O'Brien, an engagingly relaxed yet persistent interviewer, makes it plain from the outset that she is not looking for easy answers. . . . She reports the encouraging and the discouraging with dispassionate impartiality."

For Soledad, the praise was welcome, yet her connection to *Black in America* went beyond sheer professional interest. As a biracial woman, the chance to tackle the thorny issue of race provided the opportunity to explore her own roots.

Blacks in America

The rich history of blacks in America began centuries ago when the slave trade brought thousands of West Africans across the Atlantic Ocean to North American shores. The generations forced to work Southern plantations saw their families and their dignity destroyed by racist policies. President Abraham Lincoln ended the practice by signing the Emancipation Proclamation in 1863, but widespread prejudice continued. Still, African Americans retained their own customs and ways of life; they also fought for acceptance and equal rights.

Even before the Civil Rights Movement of the 1950s and 1960s, blacks fought and died in American wars and helped build the nation through industry, art, and intellect. While leaders such as Martin Luther King and Malcolm X became **icons**, other unsung heroes and artists paved the way for contemporary black America as well. Together, they reveal an important truth: the black experience and the American experience cannot be separated.

A quick rise through the television ranks had brought Soledad to MSNBC's weekend morning show *The Site*. This led to reports for the highly rated *Today Show* and the *NBC Nightly News*. Soledad later took a high-profile job with CNN, the all-news cable network, and its show *American Morning*. This afforded her chances to cover stories ranging from the Iraq War to Hurricane Katrina. Bright, beautiful, and driven, Soledad was quickly recognized for her on-air skills and dedication to her stories. She not only asked the hard questions, she also appeared willing to make uncommon sacrifices to follow her stories.

In late 2004, only months after giving birth to twins, Soledad traveled to Thailand to cover the aftermath of a devastating **tsunami** that killed 225,000 people. She also anchored the coverage of Palestinian leader Yasser Arafat's funeral. Soledad was everywhere, working hard to juggle a rewarding family life with the career she loved.

Awards followed. The Katrina team, of which she was a part, won a George Foster Peabody Award for excellence in journalism. Her tsunami work earned an Alfred I. DuPont Award. In 2007, Soledad also won a Gracie Allen Award for coverage of the Middle East conflict.

SETBACK AND TRIUMPH

Then, in April 2007, things changed dramatically for Soledad when CNN swiftly replaced her on *American Morning*. No longer seen as the fresh face in TV news, Soledad looked like just another ratings casualty. Even industry insiders were shocked at the sudden move.

Yet, after nearly two decades, Soledad understood the business all too well. Her new freedom allowed her to pursue the stories she found most meaningful. She worked on the documentary *Children of the Storm* with acclaimed director Spike Lee. She covered exit polling during the 2008 presidential primaries and election, and reported from the historic **inauguration** of the nation's first African-American president.

By spring 2009 she was busy preparing *Black in America 2*. For Soledad, the importance of the project was self-evident:

> **"The story of black people in this country needs to be told—a wide range of stories—some of successful blacks, stories of some who are struggling. We interview corporate execs and recovering addicts. . . . We have lots of stories that make up who we are—and guess what, we're more than rappers and ballers and secretaries of state (though we are that too)."**

After she was replaced on *American Morning*, Soledad had the freedom to work with Spike Lee on *Children of Storm*, a CNN documentary that focused on the lives of New Orleans teenagers two years after Hurricane Katrina.

The second installment of the highly regarded series marked the latest triumph for one of America's top broadcast journalists. After years of globe-trotting and reporting from the world's hot spots, Soledad found her most important and personal story waiting on American shores. But like so many of the African Americans she interviewed, her own story defied any simple explanation.

A
DIFFERENT
LOOK

SOLEDAD O'BRIEN'S JOURNEY TO THE TOP of her profession began decades ago. Her close-knit family, stellar education, and innate talent provided the spark. But none guaranteed her success in the fast-paced, competitive world of TV journalism. For that, Soledad would have to work long hours, weather occasional disappointment, and hope to catch a lucky break.

AN INTERRACIAL MARRIAGE

Soledad's parents, Estella and Edward, met in 1959. Estella grew up on the island of Cuba; her family also included ancestors of African stock. Edward hailed from Toowoomba, Australia, the white son of Irish immigrants. They both went to school at Johns Hopkins University in Baltimore but didn't meet there. As devout

Working Mother magazine cover, May 2001

Working Mother

GROWN KIDS SPEAK OUT

"My Mom Worked (and I turned out great!)"

NBC's Soledad O'Brien with her mom and 4-month-old daughter

THE TRICK TO PAYING FOR COLLEGE

NET A JOB
Best Ways To Find Work On The Web

NEVER SAY DIET
How To Handle Your Kid's Weight

MAY 2001

$2.99US $3.99CAN

WorkingMother.com

SAFIA KHALIL RIZVI
MOTHER OF THE YEAR

Soledad appears with her mother and baby on the cover of *Working Mother* magazine. As the product of an interracial marriage, Soledad and her siblings didn't look like the other children at school. She always felt different until she went to Harvard University, a college that was more accepting of diversity.

Catholics, Estella and Edward attended **mass** at a local church each day. Once, Edward noticed Estella sitting in one of the church pews nearby. After the service, he offered to drive her home. Estella politely declined. But the next day, Edward offered again. Again, she said no. In time, Edward's persistence paid off; Estella finally accepted a ride. The couple became engaged less than a year later.

Rather than marry in Baltimore, Estella and Edward headed an hour south to Washington, D.C. In the early 1960s, interracial marriage laws were freer in the nation's capital.

Challenging Miscegenation Laws

As far back as the 1660s, early settlers to the New World banned interracial marriage. The word **miscegenation**, coined by anti-Abolitionists in 1860s, struck fear into those who believed that mixing races would weaken pure, white blood. Many states passed laws banning interracial relationships.

Then in 1958, Richard Loving and Mildred Jeter traveled to Washington, D.C., to make their love legal. But when the married couple returned to Virginia, one of 15 states that outlawed the practice, police raided their home and charged them with defying race laws. Mildred, of African- and Native-American descent, and Richard, a white man, took their case to the Supreme Court. In 1967, the ban on interracial marriage was overturned and the court wrote,

66 Under our Constitution, the freedom to marry, or not marry, a person of another race resides with the individual and cannot be infringed by the State. 99

Today, seven percent of marriages in the United States are interracial.

GROWING UP ON LONG ISLAND

After getting married, Estella and Edward O'Brien moved to Smithtown, New York, on Long Island's North Shore. By now, Edward and Estella had become educators. Estella taught in a local public school; Edward worked as a college professor in electrical engineering. Their first child, Maria, was born in 1961, followed by Cecelia in 1962, Tony in 1963, and Estella in 1964. Maria de la Soledad Teresa O'Brien came into the world on September 19, 1966.

Her brother, Orestes, followed a year later. The name Soledad means "The Blessed Virgin of Solitude."

Estella and Edward provided their growing family with love, support, and an abiding sense of faith. But growing up in the 1960s and '70s included its share of hardship, particularly for biracial children. Soledad and her siblings looked like few others in their elementary and middle schools, or Smithville High School. As she later said in an interview,

Mildred and Richard Loving challenged laws against interracial marriage in the Supreme Court case *Loving* v. *Virginia*. At the time Soledad's parents got together, some of the miscegenation rules were still in place, so they married in Washington, D.C., where the laws were freer.

❝I consider myself black primarily, and Latina sort of secondarily. . . . I knew I was different from my early childhood. I knew I would never date anybody in high school. Nobody wants to date somebody who looks different. . . . It would be incorrect to say I had a very traumatic experience. . . . Once I went to college, where differences are more accepted, people didn't care much.**❞**

For Soledad and each of her siblings, college was Harvard University in Cambridge, Massachusetts. Soledad found the prestigious Ivy League institution a less judgmental environment than Long Island. She excelled in school and majored in English literature. But her interests were not limited to reading and writing. Soledad also studied science by taking pre-med courses and briefly considered becoming a doctor.

FIRST TASTE OF JOURNALISM

In 1989, Soledad's interest in medicine led her to KISS-FM radio in Boston, where she landed a job hosting the medical talk shows *Second Opinion* and *Health Week in Review*. The work gave Soledad her first taste of journalism, and she liked it. At about the same time, she won an **internship** with Boston television station WBZ-TV, a NBC **affiliate**. Producers took an interest in her in part because of her course work in biology and chemistry. But according to Soledad, the work proved less than glamorous:

❝I did an internship, so I took staples out of walls, answered phones and fetched coffee. And then I got hired as assistant to the medical reporter, which meant I took staples out of her walls, answered her phone and fetched her coffee.**❞**

Before Soledad had even finished college, she was working for the WBZ-TV full-time. She dropped out of Harvard and took her first position in TV news as a researcher for WBZ's medical reporter.

Soledad's first taste of journalism took place in this WBZ-TV studio in Boston. Beginning as an intern, she became a researcher and then started writing and producing news stories. Soon she was being noticed for her hard work and ambition, which led to her next career move.

By 1990, Soledad's career in Boston was thriving. She had moved beyond the title of researcher and moved on to writing news stories and producing them for the air. Working mostly behind the scenes, she made phone calls, organized schedules, and helped the stations' reporters get their stories. WBZ built her confidence. But her Boston days would be short-lived, as bigger things awaited.

Chapter

3

FAST START

BY EARLY 1991, SOLEDAD O'BRIEN'S WORK FOR Boston's WBZ-TV was coming to an end. The brainy 25-year-old had proven to be hard-working, ambitious, and attractive. But many newcomers have the same qualities. Soledad would once again have to prove that she was prepared to take the next big step in her career.

Based on her WBZ-TV credentials, Soledad was offered a job at NBC News as a researcher and producer for its science correspondent, Robert Bazell. Network news is national; her work would be seen all across the country, giving her far more exposure than she had in Boston.

So for two years, Soledad lived and labored in New York City as a field producer. She produced stories on cancer, computers, and cell phones, among others. Her work often appeared on the *NBC Nightly News* and the *Today Show,* two of the best-known programs in television.

Soledad appears as a correspondent for KRON in San Francisco. After a fast start as a producer for NBC News in New York, she still wanted to appear in front of the cameras. So she jumped at the chance to work for KRON as a reporter.

She had made it to the big leagues, but something was missing. Soledad yearned for on-camera exposure, yet the opportunities at NBC were limited for an unproven on-air talent.

HEADING WEST

In 1993, NBC affiliate KRON in San Francisco offered Soledad a chance to appear on camera. She leaped at the chance and flew across the country to take the job. Straight away, she earned her reporting stripes by covering local stories and honing her leadership skills as the East Bay bureau chief. One of her early successes was co-hosting KRON's *The Know Zone*, for which she won an Emmy Award in 1995. She remembers the show's focus:

> **"It wasn't strictly a science and technology show for kids, but it kind of had a kid bent to it. We covered science in a conversational tone and tried to find unusual ways to explain things."**

With her career taking off, Soledad turned to personal matters. She and Bradley Raymond had dated since college and in 1995 she and the investment banker married. Professionally, she also gained experience on *The Next Step*, a Discovery Channel program. As the "Sun Microsystems Infogal," her job was to provide basic story facts while looking pretty.

Such positions in TV news are not uncommon, as beautiful women are often highlighted by networks to try and attract more ratings. Despite the **sexist** title, Soledad retained her dignity through her poise and wit. Yet she determined not remain an infogal forever.

NEW CHANNEL, NEW CHANCE

In early 1996, NBC officials made a major announcement: the network would join forces with software giant Microsoft on a news channel that they hoped would rival industry leader CNN. The channel's name—MSNBC—combined the names of its two parent companies.

In 1993 Soledad headed west to San Francisco, California. She found success as a co-host of *The Know Zone*, covering science in interesting ways, and she received an Emmy Award for her work in 1995. She also appeared on the Discovery Channel's program *The Next Step*.

Recognizing an exceptional opportunity, Soledad lobbied for a job as host of the new MSNBC show *The Site* and got it. On the nightly show, Soledad interviewed guests about new Web sites and software and talked technology with a cartoon character named Dev Null. Despite the silly premise, the job gave her national exposure. She also helped disprove a 1990s myth that women and technology did not go together, as she told *The Detroit News*:

“The web is feminizing the entire industry. It's a very collaborative medium and women work well collaboratively. It's not just some computer geek sitting alone at his desk. It's people all around the world contributing.”

Viewers quickly warmed to Soledad's fresh face and sense of humor. Male viewers, especially, found her an attractive presence,

Soledad talks about Web sites and software on *The Site*, including an "interview" with cartoon character Dev Null. The program, which appeared on the new TV channel MSNBC, helped Soledad gain national exposure and prove that women could be knowledgeable and good-humored about computers and technology.

nicknaming her "Goddess of the Geeks." *The Washington Post* referred to her as "television's first cyberbabe."

The Internet in the 1990s

The origins of the Internet stretch back to at least the 1960s, when it was used in universities. But in the 1990s the World Wide Web became a global revolution. One of the earliest browsers, called Mosaic, made entrance easier and more reliable.

By 1994, skyrocketing sales of personal home computers led to a greater public awareness of the resource. Soon, companies like Microsoft and Apple provided user-friendly ways to access the growing "information superhighway."

At the time, people connected to the Internet through their phone lines. But dial-up proved slow and engineers began developing faster ways to surf the Web. By now anything and everything can be found on the Internet, with content growing 100 percent each year. As Web sites mushroomed, so did users. Today, at least 1.5 billion people use the Internet.

WEEKEND WARRIOR

In April 1997, PBS affiliate WNET hired Soledad to host a news magazine called *Imaging America*. Each episode took an hour-long tour of an American city. Early programs looked at Phoenix, Arizona, and Portland, Oregon. Soledad enjoyed researching each city and talking to ordinary Americans:

> **"I loved doing this type of show. . . . I like having a full hour to tell a story, and also not intruding into the story as a journalist—the people in this show tell the story of Phoenix themselves—I'm just there to ask questions and connect the dots."**

That fall, *The Site* ended its run and NBC executives were looking for bigger and better ways to use their new star. She became fill-in anchor for *The News with Brian Williams*. Then in July 1999, she began co-anchoring the *Weekend Today* show. Her co-anchor was veteran journalist David Bloom.

Soledad and David Bloom appear as co-hosts of NBC's *Weekend Today*. The show covered serious stories like the space shuttle disaster and the invasion of Iraq. Soledad was shocked and saddened when David died unexpectedly while on assignment in Iraq.

Soledad was fast becoming a household name. Her own household was growing too. On October 23, 2000, she and Brad welcomed daughter Sofia Elizabeth, their first child. Two years later, on March 20, 2002, Soledad gave birth to daughter Cecelia.

On *Weekend Today*, the stories of the day were often dramatic and intense like the one on Saturday, February 1, 2003. That day the space shuttle Columbia prepared to return home after completing its mission. But upon reentry—at 9:05 A.M.—Columbia disintegrated over Palestine, Texas. Seven astronauts died.

Soledad and David Bloom covered nearly every angle of the disaster on *Weekend Today*, but the shuttle tragedy was soon displaced by another news event: the invasion of Iraq launched by the United States on March 20, 2003. Bloom immediately flew to Iraq to get an on-the-ground view of the military operations. His up-to-the-minute reports from the battlefield became an important feature of NBC's coverage of the war.

Journalists and the Iraq War

On the eve of the Iraq War in 2003, a number of network news organizations made a unique pact with the federal government: the Department of Defense would give journalists the closest view of war ever; journalists would sign a contract restricting what they could report and when they could report it. Such agreements placed dozens of news people in the backs of tanks, where they presented readers or viewers detailed accounts of the invasion of Iraq and the fall of Baghdad.

But these so-called "embedded" reporters also depended on the American military for their safety and security. This, critics suggested, threatened the journalists' ability to remain neutral or get the entire story. According to reporter Bob Steele,

66 There's nothing wrong with having respect in our hearts for the men and women who are fighting this war . . . the key is to make sure those beliefs don't color reporting. 99

On April 5, while traveling with 3rd Infantry Division, David Bloom collapsed and died. Experts speculated that the hours of crouching in cramped military vehicles may have led to Deep Vein Thrombosis, or DVT. The blood clot that results can travel to the lungs and cause death. The news stunned Soledad, who lost her co-host and friend. Little did she know that more change was coming, whether she liked it or not.

RISE
AND SHINE

BY MID-2003, SOLEDAD O'BRIEN FACED ONE of the most important decisions of her professional life. For nearly 12 years, she had worked for NBC News or one of its affiliates, but the network offered few new opportunities. Viewers knew and liked her work on morning television, but chances for a daily anchoring spot were rare.

CNN's *American Morning* program premiered on September 12, 2001, the day after the worst terrorist attack in American history. The show's original host, Paula Zahn, was a certified star of morning television, but by early 2003 she wanted to host an evening program. CNN executives looking for her replacement had taken note of Soledad's work on NBC. That spring they made her an offer few TV journalists could refuse.

Soledad appears as a co-host of CNN's *American Morning*. She was thrilled to anchor a daily news show and especially enjoyed the interviews of people affected by current events. But the job meant getting up at 4:00 A.M., which made it hard to juggle work and her growing family.

MOVING TO CNN

Soledad began her duties on *American Morning* in July 2003, co-hosting the show with Bill Hemmer. The program offered more news and less pure entertainment than *Today* or *Good Morning America*, and Soledad and Hemmer found an easy rapport that quickly became popular with viewers. They introduced stories, interviewed a variety of guests, and did for cable TV what those others morning shows did for the networks.

Soledad also got to do what she loved best: ask questions and explore the lives of other people. She covered the biggest news stories of the day, including the ongoing war in Iraq. But personally, her biggest story was still in development. Soledad was pregnant with twins. And on August 30, 2004, Charlie and Jackson joined the O'Brien-Raymond family.

Then, soon after returning from maternity leave, Soledad covered the catastrophic South Asian tsunami in December 2004. CNN flew only a handful of anchors to one of the disaster zones in Thailand, and Soledad was one of them. There, she witnessed firsthand the devastation that resulted in the death of more than 225,000 people in 11 countries. She met real people whose lives had been forever transformed by nature's brute force. She couldn't help but be moved by their struggles to survive and rebuild their broken lives. She later spoke of the best part of her job:

> **❝I love to be in the field running around and talking to people. You just learn so much. I get to . . . be inspired by them. I love to be moved and impressed by people . . . who do remarkable things.❞**

MORE CHANGES

Back home, Soledad and Bill Hemmer continued their hosting duties, but CNN executives were unhappy. Most television programming is driven by advertising dollars. The more people watch a show, the more a network can charge advertisers to run their commercials. Despite Soledad and Bill Hemmer's hard work,

Soledad introduces serious news stories on *American Morning*. The program's coverage was less entertainment oriented and included events like the Asian tsunami, the war in Iraq, and the search for international terrorists. Soledad thrived on presenting the stories she discovered as a field reporter.

few people watched *American Morning* compared to other shows in the same time slot.

Executives called for changes to the program. They began by replacing Hemmer. While Soledad remained the network's best hope for higher morning ratings, she was now joined each morning by veteran science reporter Miles O'Brien. In a statement, CNN's president Jonathan Klein said that he wanted to improve the on-air chemistry of the show and implied that Hemmer had a hard time sharing the spotlight.

Soledad and Miles O'Brien became co-hosts of *American Morning* in 2005. CNN executives hoped the chemistry between Soledad and Miles would attract viewers and improve ratings. The two got down to business and soon were challenged by some major news stories.

Miles O'Brien, on the other hand, was seen by network executives as generous and supportive of his co-anchors. While having the same last name became the stuff of jokes early in their time together, Soledad and her new co-host could be serious when they needed to be and meshed well. Little did Soledad know that soon she would be reporting from one of the largest disasters in American history.

HURRICANE KATRINA

In August 2005, Hurricane Katrina slammed the Gulf Coast of the United States, flooding streets and ripping homes apart. Hundreds of thousands of people were displaced; thousands perished. Again, Soledad traveled to the scene and reported on the shattered lives of those left in the storm's wake.

The Deadly Storm

When Hurricane Katrina made landfall in New Orleans, Louisiana, on August 29, 2005, many believed the worst was over. But in the hours after the massive storm the levees that protected the below-sea-level city failed in 50 places due to heavy rainfall and the high waters of Lake Pontchartrain. Soon, 80 percent of the fabled city was under water.

Residents who refused to leave or had no transportation now found escape impossible. Mostly poor and black and from the city's Lower Ninth Ward, thousands of people were stranded with little food and drinkable water. In desperation, many made their way to the convention center or the Superdome where they spent three days baking in the hot summer sun. Eventually, the Coast Guard and Air National Guard did reach the suffering, rescuing over 33,000 people. But Katrina killed 1,836 others, making it one of the deadliest storms in American history.

On September 2, 2005, Soledad interviewed **FEMA** Director Mike Brown via satellite from Baton Rouge. The federal response to the hurricane had come under intense analysis, and many Americans questioned whether their government was doing enough to help the struggling citizens of Louisiana and Mississippi. With a majority of the city under water, explosions and fires now raging, and armed bandits roaming the streets of New Orleans, Soledad pelted Brown with questions:

When did he become aware of the thousands stranded at the convention center? Why was CNN getting better information on the deteriorating situation than FEMA? Why was it that after four

New Orleans is largely under water after Hurricane Katrina struck in 2005. Soledad impressed viewers with her coverage of the ruined city and its people. In particular, her interview with the director of FEMA raised important questions about the effectiveness of the government's response to natural disasters.

days no food or water was being dropped by helicopter to those in need? The exchange between Brown and Soledad became testy, but Soledad pressed him for answers. Yet to most Americans watching the interview, those answers proved unsatisfactory. Ten days after the broadcast, Brown resigned.

WORKING MOM

After three years, Soledad was used to the daily grind of morning television. She rose at 4 A.M., got to the CNN studio by 4:30 or 5 A.M., went on the air at 6:00 A.M., and finished her working day in the early afternoon. The odd hours afforded her quality time with her husband and four young children, but she found her schedule hectic and challenging at times.

Although she loved her job as one of the most high-profile journalists on television, the pressures of being a working mom sometimes got her, as she said in an interview in 2006:

> **“I think it's sort of feeling pulled in all directions and feeling, frankly, very stressed all the time. . . . It's physically hard, it's emotionally hard. Some days you feel like you're giving everybody a C minus on all fronts, and that doesn't feel very good.”**

Yet motherhood, she said, taught her patience and reminded her how lucky she was to have healthy children and a thriving career. She had time to take her kids to doctors' appointments and could cook dinner almost every night.

NAACP AWARD

More than ever, Soledad was earning the respect of her peers. During her many years in the business, she had built a solid reputation as an extraordinary TV journalist, and industry watchers wondered when she would land her next big story. But in 2007, Soledad herself became the story. She accepted the prestigious Gracie Award from the American Women in Radio and Television. In March, she flew to Los Angeles, California, to accept the NAACP President's Award for special achievement and distinguished public service.

Upon receiving her award at the 38th annual NAACP Image Awards, Soledad walked to the microphone. She wore a red, strapless dress for the occasion and waited for the applause to subside before speaking:

> **"I have been absolutely blessed, and it is a privilege to cover some of *the* most important stories of our time. And, too, at times, be a voice for people who have no voice; shine a light on places that sometimes people who prefer to ignore; to ask the uncomfortable questions."**

The NAACP and Other President's Award Winners

With more than half a million members, the National Association for the Advancement of Colored People (NAACP) remains one of the nation's premier defenders of civil rights. Founded in 1909 by a group of reformers that included W.E.B. Du Bois, Ida B. Wells, and Henry Moscowitz, the NAACP fought for racial equality during some of the darkest days in American history.

Its yearly Image Awards ceremony pays tribute to outstanding achievements by people of color. The President's Award, one of the most prestigious, is given to a person of special achievement and "distinguished public service." Previous winners include jazz legend Ella Fitzgerald, former secretary of state Condoleezza Rice, tennis champions Venus and Serena Williams, former president Bill Clinton, and boxing great Muhammad Ali.

Soledad also spoke of an exciting new project at CNN in which young survivors of Hurricane Katrina were given video cameras to document their lives in the aftermath of the devastating storm. The project, in its early stages, revealed both heartbreak and hope, said Soledad. She then asked those in the audience and the millions of viewers watching at home not to forget the people of New Orleans and all along the Gulf Coast. For a night, at least, the reporter became an advocate for those less fortunate. It would not be the last time.

A glamorous Soledad accepts the NAACP President's Award onstage during 2007 NAACP Image Awards. As she thanked the group for her award for distinguished public service, Soledad said she was lucky to cover many important news stories and to throw light on subjects some people would rather ignore.

ON THE OUTS

In April 2007, Soledad's professional world was turned upside down. In a stunning but not unexpected move, CNN executives announced they were replacing Soledad and Miles O'Brien as *American Morning* co-anchors. The reason: poor ratings.

Kiran Chetry and John Roberts became the new faces of the *American Morning* show. Soledad, the network announced, would become a "special correspondent," hosting a weekly program called *CNN: Special Investigations Unit.* Miles O'Brien would return to covering science news.

Soledad stood at a crossroads. Her eight-year run as an anchor ended. Although her role on CNN was changing, hers remained a vital voice. She began giving keynote speeches across the country, speaking at Cornell and Bryant Universities and participating in the CTAM Summit, a telecommunications gathering, in July 2007.

KATRINA, TWO YEARS LATER

At CNN, Soledad turned her gaze toward longer programming. In particular, she continued work on the Hurricane Katrina project she had first mentioned at the NAACP Awards.

In January, Soledad teamed with acclaimed film director Spike Lee to give 11 teens video cameras. Soledad remembered the filmmaker's advice to the young people:

Spike Lee

Atlanta-born Shelton (Spike) Lee found his passion early. At 20, the young African American made his first film while still attending Morehouse College. At New York University Film School he won a Student Academy Award for *Joe's Bed-Stuy Barbershop: We Cut Heads.* In 1986, Spike scraped together $160,000 to make *She's Gotta Have It.* It became his first feature film, grossed $700,000 at the box office, and took Spike's filmmaking to the next level.

Bigger features followed, as did controversy. Through the late 1980s and into the early 1990s, Spike's now-classic films *Do the Right Thing* and *Malcolm X* challenged America's views on race. These films provided insight into the experiences of blacks and whites, as well as their struggles to understand one another. Spike Lee continues writing and directing feature films and documentaries that ask important questions about what it means to be an American in the 21st century.

Soledad talks with film director Spike Lee about their CNN documentary, *Children of the Storm*. Two years after Hurricane Katrina, she and Spike gave video cameras to 11 New Orleans teenagers to help them document how their lives had been changed by the devastation of their home town.

❝On the day we distributed the cameras, Spike Lee told the kids to 'just go out and shoot, tape is cheap.' . . . these kids have taught us all a powerful, infinitely valuable lesson that will stay with me forever.❞

In August, 2007, CNN broadcast *Children of the Storm*. Among the young people providing up-close and personal views of life after the storm was 18-year-old Amanda Hill. She and her grandmother

Dolores lost their home when Katrina hit. On her tape, Amanda spoke of waking at 3 A.M. to the sounds of her grandmother crying because she didn't know whether she'd be able to feed the two of them. Dolores, said Amanda, even considered suicide. Months

Shantia Reneau is one of several young people from New Orleans who shared their personal stories of Hurricane Katrina's aftermath in *Children of the Storm*. Shantia eventually enrolled in Southeastern Louisiana University. Soledad was impressed by the teens' dedication to getting on with life and their positive attitudes about the future.

after Katrina, the two women returned to St. Bernard Parish outside New Orleans. Dolores tried to make ends meet by working at a local McDonald's.

Another teen, Shantia Reneau, had to put her dream of attending college on hold. Two years after Katrina, her family still lived in a FEMA trailer. Any money they had they put into rebuilding their house in the city's Lower Ninth Ward. For Shantia, college would have to wait.

Fifteen-year-old Deshawn Dabney wondered whether he'd live to see another birthday. Gang violence had increased since Katrina, and on video Deshawn spoke of the shooting death of his neighbor, Anthony Placide. The murder occurred only a few hundred feet from Deshawn's house.

The stories contained in *Children of the Storm* moved Soledad and had a profound impact on her own life, as she said when promoting the program:

> **"The one thing that amazed me most of all was that they were so positive. They were all clearly dedicated to sticking it out and getting on with their lives and having New Orleans be part of their lives in some capacity."**

Less than a year later, Soledad would again be inspired by the unique and complex stories of everyday Americans. But this time, the people she met echoed her experience as a biracial woman.

Chapter

5

~ ❀ ~

STORIES
WITH
MEANING

SOLEDAD HAD COVERED PRESIDENTS, popes, Cuban refugees, and terrorist attacks. But her ethnicity and upbringing were never far from her mind. These things defined her and made her the person she was. But over the next year, her work would force her to reconsider just about everything she knew about herself and the lives of other African Americans.

At CNN, Soledad was now a **free agent**. No longer tied to the repetition of early morning hosting duties, she relished her new role at CNN as host of its special investigations unit. Now, she could explore a subject in depth. The hours agreed with her too. Gone was the 3 A.M. wake-up call. The busy mother of four could now concentrate more on her family as well as cover some of the most interesting news stories of the day.

Soledad O'Brien
Anchor
Correspondent, Special Investigations Unit

cnnobservations.com

Soledad appears as anchor and correspondent of CNN's Special Investigation Unit. Once she left her job as an early morning host, Soledad found herself with a new assignment that meant she could present in-depth coverage of important stories and spend more time with her family.

FOCUS ON RACE

CNN producers were always on the lookout for innovative programming. In looking at the stories covered on CNN and elsewhere, executives found that many of the stories dealing with black Americans appeared negative. From this perception came the idea for *Black in America*. Producers envisioned an epic series that examined the successes and struggles faced by black men, women, and families 40 years after the death of Martin Luther King, Jr.

Martin Luther King, Jr. and the Civil Rights Movement

Martin Luther King grew up the son and grandson of church pastors. In 1954, he became pastor of Dexter Avenue Baptist Church in Montgomery, Alabama. Just one year later, when seamstress Rosa Parks refused to give up her seat at the front of the bus to a white passenger and was arrested, King led a boycott of the bus company, which lasted 382 days.

But victory came at a cost: King and his family were under constant threat. Yet for 13 more years, King led the civil rights movement using the nonviolent philosophy of Indian leader Mahatma Gandhi. King led protests, spoke out against racial injustice, and wrote eloquently about the stain of **bigotry**. His dream of all people living free of prejudice and injustice remains the dream of millions.

According to vice president and senior executive producer of CNN productions Mark Nelson, the idea for the series began as a quest for diversity. He believed that because of its importance in American life, the issue of race deserved closer study. He and fellow producers discussed possible hosts for the program but quickly settled on Soledad. Who, they wondered, could better embody the complexity and variety of the African-American experience than Soledad? Once on board, Soledad became convinced the series would have an impact on viewers:

"The series has critical information for people of all races—the 'Black in America' experience is an American story. This is a raw and intimate look at stories that everyone will be able to relate to."

Civil rights leader Martin Luther King, Jr. gives his famous "I Have a Dream" speech during the March on Washington, 1963. Soledad was proud to be selected to host *Black in America*, a CNN series that studied the issue of race 40 years after the death of Dr. King.

APRIL 1968

Since civil rights leader Martin Luther King, Jr. partly inspired the series, producers believed it only appropriate that his assassination take center stage in the first episode of *Black in America*. Thus, Soledad traveled to Memphis, Tennessee. There, at the Lorraine Motel on April 4, 1968, King was gunned down on a balcony outside his room.

Soledad stands on the balcony of the motel where Martin Luther King, Jr. was assassinated, during "Eyewitness to Murder: The King Assassination," the first installment of CNN's *Black in America*. Soledad interviewed people who knew both King and his killer and set the serious tone for the rest of the special series.

Standing outside room 306 of the Lorraine Motel, Soledad introduced this dark chapter of American history in "Eyewitness to Murder." For two hours, the program charted King's history but paid special attention to the days leading up to his death, the assassination itself, and the conspiracy theories that followed.

Soledad's interview with former Atlanta mayor Andrew Young revealed King's sense of humor. According to Young, King often joked that the one of his friends should take the bullet if anyone ever tried to kill him. King told them that if they did so he would preach an excellent **sermon** at their funeral. But Young also noted that the civil rights leader believed that assassination was a very real possibility, especially after the murder of President John F. Kennedy in 1963.

Soledad also interviewed Jerry Ray, brother of convicted King assassin James Earl Ray. Soledad's reporting revealed Ray's movements before and after the assassination, and her probing questions helped reveal many details of King's murder that were little known to the public. Reverend Billy Kyles spoke to Soledad about the night before King's death. As King gave a speech to striking sanitation workers, a storm outside caused the shutters in the building to bang. Each time they did, said Kyles, King would suddenly turn and look behind him, thinking the shutters could be gunfire.

While "Eyewitness to Murder" did not settle the question of whether there was a conspiracy to kill Martin Luther King, Jr., it did remind Americans of the legacy of the civil rights leader and set the tone for a contemporary look at black America.

BLACK MEN

Another episode titled "The Black Men" took a hard look at the role black fathers play in their families and in American society at large. Soledad offered the sobering statistic that the number of children born to black, unwed mothers has tripled to nearly 70 percent since the 1960s. In many cases, the fathers of those children abandon their women and children. Her work on the program gave Soledad a fresh perspective. She said,

> ❝What I learned was that in our nation we have a lot of work to do. The picture of African Americans in this country needs to be a more diverse picture. It's not the four images we know; it's the thirty images. . . . We are a wide range of things.❞

Soledad and CNN producer Stan Wilson also visited San Quentin prison in Oakland, California, to talk with inmates.

An inmate shows Soledad his high school diploma during the filming of "The Black Men," an episode from *Black in America*. The interview showed the contrast between a convicted felon who found new direction in prison and other men who were still dealing drugs on the street.

One of them, Chris Shurn, had entered the prison when he was 21 for crack cocaine possession and a weapons violation. Like the nearly 1 million other black men incarcerated in the United States, Shurn had little direction and few prospects. But during his four years behind bars, he hit the books, earning his **GED**, and nearly completed a college associate's degree. Upon his release, he held down a job at Goodwill. But at seven dollars an hour, Shurn had trouble making ends meet; when he lost his job, he wondered how he would continuing support his girlfriend and her daughter.

Soledad's interviews revealed the desperation that young black men often face. Forty years after King's death, opportunities for success had improved, but poverty and crime still defined the lives of so many. Khalid Carter, she found, embodied the plight of millions of black men. As a drug dealer in Baltimore, Maryland, Carter worked 16 hours a day, hustling for cash. Soledad returned with him to the street corner where he earned his living, and where he nearly lost his life in a shooting.

Soledad interviews an inmate at San Quentin prison during "The Black Men." Her conversations emphasized that while some opportunities for success were better than before, poverty, lack of education, and crime often added up to be a death sentence for many black men.

According to Soledad, 93 percent of murder victims in Baltimore are African American. Carter was shot and taken to the nearest hospital where Dr. Carnell Cooper saved him. Dr. Cooper started the Violence Intervention Project (VIP), a program that helped young men train for better jobs and earn their high school diplomas.

THE BLACK EXPERIENCE

Never one to shy away from uncomfortable issues, Soledad also talked to author Joseph C. Phillips, who published a book entitled *He Talk Like a White Boy*. She and Phillips discussed the varying definitions of what it means to be a black man in the United States today.

He Talk Like a White Boy

Joseph C. Phillips found early fame when he appeared on TV's *The Cosby Show* in the 1980s. But his life truly changed when he was in eighth grade and a black classmate commented on his speech by saying, "He talk like a white boy." Those words became the title of his 2006 book, which wrestles with questions of racial identity in the 21st century.

In the book, Phillips attempts to reach beyond what he considers less important issues like how a person talks. Instead, he says, he is far more concerned about how members of the black community raise their children and carry on their relationships. But Phillips is also aware that the way he talks, as well as his conservative beliefs, put him in the minority of the African-American community. Still, he remains determined to prove that there is no such thing as *the* black experience; there are black experiences, none more or less authentic than any other.

Later, Soledad interviewed James Warren and Kenneth Roy Allen. The men attended Little Rock Central High School Class and graduated in 1968. Desegregated in 1957, the school became a lightning rod for arguments over equality and discrimination. Warren succeeded early, becoming a teacher and rising to assistant superintendent of schools. Classmate Allen became a petty thief and drug addict but eventually pieced his life back together.

Soledad was moved by the storied she heard and inspired by the people she interviewed,

Soledad talks to Joseph C. Phillips, author of *He Talk Like a White Boy,* and his family during filming of "The Black Men." Soledad was inspired by the many types of black experience she found and the positive ways the people she interviewed faced life every day.

"Every story has its sad side, but in the aftermath, you see the optimism and tenacity. The people who open their homes, their lives, their checkbooks . . . if you can't be inspired by that, you have a heart of stone."

BLACK FAMILIES

Another *Black in America* episode, "The Black Woman and Family," featured the ever-evolving role of black women in American life. One key conversation Soledad had was with *Essence* magazine editor Angela Burt-Murray in which the two discussed black women and interracial relationships.

Specifically, Burt-Murray spoke of the high rates of achievement for black women in the 21st century. Later, Soledad echoed these thoughts:

> **❝The numbers of women who have great success—black women with great success—are higher than ever. So as difficult as the challenge has always been, we are doing well. Could we be doing better? Absolutely.❞**

According to Burt-Murray, some black women grappled with whether or not they needed a partner to feel complete. And when they did seek a partner, African-American women were more open than ever to finding a relationship outside their race, if necessary.

Soledad also interviewed the African-American Rand family when she and her CNN crew attended their massive family reunion in Atlanta. When the program appeared on CNN, North Carolina state senator Tony Rand watched the episode and realized that the white Rands and the black Rands had a common ancestor. They were family.

MAKING A DIFFERENCE

By mid-2008, Soledad was in a journalistic groove, reporting for CNN's *Behind the Scenes* series. These were the stories that mattered to her and in which she felt she could bring her own unique perspective.

In one episode, Soledad followed 30 Brooklyn teens on a volunteer mission to South Africa. Their group, *Journey for Change*, served HIV/AIDS orphans. Malaak Compton-Rock, wife of comedian Chris Rock, organized the effort. The idea behind the trip was to provide American teens perspective on their lives and remind them of the many opportunities they have at home—free public education, food, and the chance to broaden their knowledge.

One of the teens, Latoya Massie, survives on food stamps and a government support check. But the utter poverty she witnessed in Johannesburg surprised even her. One day during the trip, she and her travel mates were given money to go shopping for some of the

Soledad poses with members of the Rand family at their family reunion in 2007. Both the white and black Rands are descended from a white farmer and slave owner in the 1800s. The Rands were featured on "The Black Woman and Family," which examined the evolving role of black women.

families they had met. They loaded their shopping carts with rice, tea, diapers, blankets, and anything else they could think of and delivered the goods to 12 families in the Soweto section of the city.

ELECTION 2008

Although Soledad's travel schedule kept her largely uninvolved with coverage of the 2008 presidential election, she and CNN's Bill Schneider did host the statistics part of the network's primary coverage. She also conducted the first in-depth interviews with the wife of Democratic hopeful Barack Obama. Soledad described Michelle Obama as thoughtful and passionate—a career woman willing to fully support her husband in his quest for the nation's highest office.

On January 19, 2009, Soledad hosted a commemorative broadcast of Martin Luther King's legendary "I Have a Dream" speech. The next day, she joined co-hosts Anderson Cooper, John King, and Wolf Blitzer in covering the inauguration of Barack Obama as the 44th president of the United States.

Soledad holds the first in-depth interviews of Michelle Obama during the 2008 presidential election. Her coverage of President Obama's inauguration and her work on *Black in America 2* were especially meaningful to Soledad because of her biracial background.

Barack Obama: The First Biracial President

On January 20, 2009, Barack Hussein Obama took the oath of office to become the first biracial president of the United States. For Obama, son of a Kenyan father and a Kansas mother, it was the end of one incredible journey and the beginning of another.

Born in Hawaii in 1961, Obama and his remarried mother moved to Indonesia when he was six. He later returned to Hawaii to be raised by his maternal grandparents. Obama attended college in Los Angeles and New York before setting down his own roots in Chicago as a community organizer. Harvard Law School followed, as did a growing interest in public service.

In 1997, Obama was elected a state legislator; in 2004 he won a senate seat. His speech at the 2004 Democratic National Convention made him a national political superstar. Four years later, he beat rival John McCain in an electoral college landslide.

Meanwhile, Soledad was already hard at work on *Black in America 2.* The overwhelming popularity of the *Black in America* series inspired a follow-up in which Soledad investigated the potential solutions to the challenges facing African Americans. Broadcast in July 2009, the program featured Soledad's interviews with filmmaker Tyler Perry, singer John Legend, and dozens of ordinary people.

The series, perhaps the crowning achievement of her career, made it clear that Soledad O'Brien had earned the respect not only of her peers but millions of viewers. As her career headed into its third decade, Soledad also recognized that her biracial background gave a distinctive viewpoint on the stories she reported:

"I think being an outsider helps you in observing things and being sensitive to differences. But it also makes you open to a lot of perspectives, and that in a way is more important."

1966   Maria de la Soledad Teresa O'Brien born on September 19 in St. James, Long Island, to Estella, an Afro-Cuban, and Edward, an Australian of Irish descent.

1984   Enters Harvard University, majoring in English and also studys science.

1988   Begins work for NBC affiliate WBZ-TV in Boston, starting as an intern but soon is hired full-time as assistant to the station's science reporter.

Leaves Harvard before completing her degree.

1989   Hosts the radio shows *Second Opinion* and *Health Week in Review* on KISS-FM radio in Boston.

1991   Joins NBC News in New York as a field producer working with the network's science reporter.

1993   Hired by KRON-TV in San Francisco as a reporter but is soon promoted to East Bay Bureau Chief.

Co-hosts *The Know Zone* for the Discovery Channel.

1995   Marries Bradley Raymond.

Wins an Emmy for her work on *The Know Zone*.

1996   Begins hosting *The Site*, an award-winning technology program on MSNBC.

1997   Hosts the MSNBC program *Morning Blend*.

Is awarded the Hispanic Achievement Award in Communications.

1999   Begins co-anchoring NBC's *Weekend Today* with partner veteran journalist David Bloom in July.

2000   Gives birth to her first child, Sofia Elizabeth, on October 23.

Completes her bachelor's degree.

2002   Daughter Cecilia Raymond is born on March 20.

2003   Covers the Columbia space shuttle disaster and the U.S. invasion of Iraq.

Co-anchor David Bloom dies while on assignment in Iraq in April.

Moves to CNN in July to co-anchor *American Morning* with Bill Hemmer.

2004   Along with husband Brad, welcomes twins Charlie and Jackson on August 30.

Flies to Thailand to cover the aftermath of the Asian tsunami in December.

2005   Travels to London to report on the subway terrorist attacks.

In early September travels to New Orleans to cover the aftermath of Hurricane Katrina.

2006   Receives the National Urban League Women of Power Award.

2007   Accepts the NAACP President's Award.

Is removed from *American Morning* and named CNN Special Correspondent.

Children of the Storm, a project conceived by Soledad and director Spike Lee, is broadcasted on CNN in August.

2008   Anchors *Black in America*, a CNN special event.

Soledad and CNN analyst Bill Schneider crunch polling numbers during the presidential primaries and on election night in November.

2009   Broadcasts as part of the team coverage of the Barack Obama's inauguration as the 44th president of the United States.

Hosts *Black in America 2* on CNN in July.

2001   *People* magazine's 50 Most Beautiful People.

2004   *People en Español*'s 50 Most Beautiful People.

Member of the National Association of Black Journalists.

Member of the National Association of Hispanic Journalists.

Board of Directors of The Harlem School of the Arts.

Top 100 Irish Americans by *Irish Americans* magazine.

2005   Hispanic Heritage Vision Award.

Hot List by *Black Enterprise* magazine.

Groundbreaking Latina of the Year award by Catalina.

2006   The National Urban League's Women of Power Award.

2007   NAACP President's Award.

American Red Cross of Massachusetts Bay's Clara Barton Humanitarian Award.

Commencement speech at Bryant University, awarded Doctor of Humane Letters honorary degree.

Convocation speech at Cornell University's Commencement.

Commencement speech at Binghamton University.

2008   Alpha Phi Alpha fraternity's Alpha Award of Honor.

Keynote speech at the annual National Association of Student Personnel Administrators (NASPA) Conference in Boston, Massachusetts.

Johns Hopkins Bloomberg School of Public Health's Goodermote Humanitarian Award for her efforts while reporting on the devastating effects of Hurricane Katrina and the 2004 Asian Tsunami.

First annual Soledad O'Brien Freedom's Voice Award, an award created in her name by Morehouse School of Medicine.

affiliate—an organization related to a parent organization through some type of control or ownership.

bigotry—treating the members of a racial or ethnic group with hatred and intolerance.

FEMA—Federal Emergency Management Agency, which coordinates responses to disasters.

free agent—a worker who operates independently, on a freelance basis.

GED—General Equivalency Diploma; the equivalent of a high school degree.

HIV/AIDS—a deadly disease caused by a virus that attacks a person's ability to fight germs.

icon—someone widely admired and looked up to for their great deeds.

inauguration—formal induction into office.

internship—an official or formal program to provide practical experience for beginners in an occupation or profession.

mass—church service in the Roman Catholic Church and some Protestant churches.

miscegenation—a mixture of races; usually marriage between a white person and a person of another race.

patriarch—male head of a family or tribal line.

sermon—a serious speech, especially on a moral issue, usually offered in a church service.

sexist—showing discrimination based on gender, especially discrimination against women.

tsunami—very large ocean wave caused by an underwater earthquake or volcanic eruption.

Books

Neff, Thomas. *Holding Out and Hanging On: Surviving Hurricane Katrina*. Columbia, MO: University of Missouri Press, 2007.

Newkirk, Pamela, ed. *Letter from Black America*. New York: Farrar, Straus, and Giroux, 2009.

O'Brien, Soledad and Rose Marie Arce. *Latino in America*. New York: Celebra Trade, 2009.

Reardon, Nancy. *On Camera: How to Report, Anchor & Interview*. St. Louis, MO: Focal Press, 2006.

Terry, Wallace. *Missing Pages: Black Journalists of Modern America: An Oral History*. New York: Basic Books, 2007.

Periodicals

Areu, Kathy. "First Person Singular," *The Washington Post* (February 4, 2007): http://www.washingtonpost.com/wp-dyn/content/article/2007/01/30/AR2007013001326.html

Frey, Jennifer. "At Hispanic Gala, Plenty of Heart and Soledad." *The Washington Post* (October 25, 2005): p. C-1.

Krinsky, Alissa. "Soledad O'Brien On Five Years At CNN: 'Exactly The Right Thing For Me,'" *TVNewser* (July 22, 2008): http://www.mediabistro.com/tvnewser/cnn/soledad_obrien_on_five_years_at_cnn_exactly_the_right_thing_for_me_89738.asp

Lee, Felicia R. "CNN Trains Its Lens on Race." *The New York Times* (July 23, 2008): p. Arts 1.

Shales, Tom. "CNN's 'Black in America' Is an Expressive Portrait." *The Washington Post* (July 23, 2008): p. C-1.

Swartz, Kristi E. "CNN Drops Science-tech Unit and Veteran Reporter." *The Atlanta Journal Constitution* (December 4, 2008): p. B-1.

Web Sites

http://www.angelrockproject.com/arp/projects/journey_for_change.asp

Malaak Compton-Rock's Angel Rock Project calls itself an "online e-village" that promotes volunteerism and social responsibility. The site contains inspirational stories of people doing for others. It also links to dozens of service organizations for those interested in getting involved.

http://www.cnn.com/CNN/anchors_reporters/obrien.soledad.html

CNN's official website provides a good starting place for highlights in the career of Soledad O'Brien.

http://soledadobrien.info/

This elegantly organized site includes a gallery of photos taken from the red carpet as well as the television studio. It also contains a Quick Facts section and a blog for fans to post questions or comments about their favorite news personality.

http://www.cnn.com/SPECIALS/2008/black.in.america/

A companion to the widely praised CNN special hosted by Soledad, the site contains news stories and videos related to race in the United States. Readers can choose from a variety of searchable topics, including civil rights, culture and lifestyle, and parenting.

ABOUT THE AUTHOR

David Robson is the recipient of two playwriting fellowships from the Delaware Division of the Arts; his plays have been performed across the country and abroad. He is also the author of several Mason Crest titles for young readers, including *Miley Cyrus*, *Chris Rock*, *Prince*, *Randy Moss*, and *Brian Westbrook*. David holds an M.F.A. from Goddard College, an M.S. from Saint Joseph's University, and a B.A. from Temple University. He lives with his family in Wilmington, Delaware.